CONSCIOUS
'How life works'...
Journal

LOUISE L. KALLAWAY

CONSCIOUS
How life works

First published in Australia by Louise L. Kallaway 2023
louiselkallaway.com

Copyright © Louise L. Kallaway 2023
All Rights Reserved

*A catalogue record for this
book is available from the
National Library of Australia*

ISBN: 978-0-6459194-0-0 (pbk)
ISBN: 978-0-6459194-1-7 (ebk)

Typesetting and design by Publicious Book Publishing
Published in collaboration with Publicious Book Publishing
www.publicious.com.au

Front cover image: Pictrider © (shutterstock)

No part of this book may be reproduced in any form, by photocopying
or by any electronic or mechanical means, including information
storage or retrieval systems, without permission in writing from
both the copyright owner and the publisher of this book.

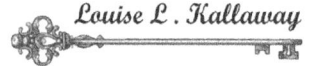

I dedicate *Conscious* to 'The individual' and its empowered place in history, and to those seekingwisdom and Higher consciousness.

Other 'Life education' books:

- Empowered – Secrets of Your Inner Child
- Defiance – Secrets of Your Midlife Crisis
- Evolving – Secrets of a child and life processes
- You and Your Inner Child Today – Journal

"Remarkable visions and genuine insights are always met with resistance. And when you start to make progress, your efforts are met with even more resistance. Products, services, career paths – whatever it is, the forces of mediocrity will align to stop you … Persist!"

Seth Godin. Marketing Guru, author.

***

The primitive *non-intellectual* survival system we inherited empowered 'The Pack' and its *'united we stand, divided we fall'* mentality, keeping our primitive cousins safe, surviving a hostile environment and a much shorter lifespan.

'The Pack' aka today's status quo, uses fear, intimidation and the threat of rejection, keeping us safe and maintaining 'order' with its *'united we stand, divided we fall'* mentality; resisting change of any kind, and so… perpetuating mediocrity.

Trouble is: 'The hardwired system' was created for a lifespan no longer than 35 years when there was no intellectual brain, no consideration for 'The individual', and no midlife problems.

Time to liberate ourselves and the 21st C. from 'The system' time forgot!

THE POWER MENU:

THE GIST i
**INTRODUCTION – MEET YOUR
'BACKSEAT DRIVER'** iii

SECTION I: THE EVOLUTIONARY SECRETS OF LIFE
1. Your personal development assessment 1
2. The Evolving Secrets of Life – Struggling?
   Feeling underpowered? Here's why! 3
3. Liberating You and the 21St Century from
   primitive survival intelligence. 6

SECTION II: BECOMING CONSCIOUS
4. Why debriefing your childhood is key to adult consciousness... 13
5. The blueprint for life – The childhood model 15
6. Benefits to living in your childhood model 18
7. Connecting with your emotional life 21
8. An understanding of the subconscious mind and survival......... 23

**SECTION III: EXAMPLES OF THE TWO TIME
ZONES IN YOUR LIFE**
9. Time zone differences 31
10. The 'Need to belong' – *an innate force* 33
11. Your 'Need to belong' and *the status quo today* 36
12. Choices 38
13. Conformity 40
14. Time and change 42
15. The 'personal' serious world of a child 44

16. Fear 46
17. Emotional dependence 48
18. Perfection 50
19. All you need is love 52

SECTION IV: UPDATING AND LIBERATING YOUR CHILDHOOD SELF-IMAGE
20. Your identity 59
21. Liking yourself today 62
22. Why liking yourself is the catalyst for change. 65

SECTION V: THE BIG PICTURE – BE INSPIRED… BECOME INSPIRING
23. How to work with your subconscious mind today 73
24. The status quo and 'The system' vs personal power 76
25. What is personal power? 80
26. Reinterpreting the 'Midlife crisis'. 81
27. The 'individual' and its place in history. 87

A TRIBUTE TO THE INNER CHILD 89
ADDENDUM – THE FAMILY – it all starts here! 93
ABOUT THE AUTHOR 97

THE GIST

We hear it all the time, don't we?

- "I've done everything I was taught to do…

- Everything I was supposed to do, should do, must do…

- I've lived by all the rules and all the standards…

- I trusted and believed this is the way life works…

Why is my life in such a mess!"

This person is stuck! unconsciously *repeating* the rules and conditioning learnt in the first half of their life and subconsciously *reacting* in present time to a similar past situation.

'Conscious' exposes one of the last frontiers as it makes sense of your life, uncomplicating and showing you what's been missing from a 'whole of life' perspective – and more.

Enjoy life's story as it unfolds, empowering and liberating new understanding.

INTRODUCTION – MEET YOUR 'BACKSEAT DRIVER'

Hello and welcome! Thank you for your trust, curiosity and courage.

Over the decades and since publishing my first book, I have become increasingly concerned with the unconsciousness of our programmed lives, especially the *reactionary repetition* of generational cycles that show up in our lives today with such learnt, observed/copied behaviour as Domestic violence. These programs/systems, lost to the vastness of time, are the very essence, the foundations that sculpt our lives, and yet, most have not been recognised as a 'forever' force today.

Life had to start from somewhere… right?

- How did we survive a hostile environment without an intellectual brain?

- How did we ensure our survival?

- Why is abandonment a primal fear?

- Was Aristotle's famous quote about the seven-year-old linked somehow?

- How and why is fear so embedded in our DNA?

- Was the subconscious mind involved in our survival? If so, how? why?

I have not re/invented the wheel! The concepts in my 'Life Education' books and journals go back to the origins of life.

My life's work has been about understanding why we repeat generational cycles, *bridging the gap* between survival intelligence and 21st Century Higher consciousness to make sense of our lives today. Understanding survival intelligence gives us a fantastic opportunity to liberate ourselves from 'The system' time forgot, giving us conscious heretofore freedom to meet our challenges/ maturing needs in the second half of our lives.

My research has found no evidence to suggest psychology plays a role in any primitive survival programs.

Chakras haven't been proven scientifically, but we 'know' when one or more is out of balance, don't we? Same with my work... there may be no scientific proof, but there is plenty of evidence. My research collated the basic survival programs evident in our lives today, e.g., fear and 'fight or flight' reactions. These 'set-in-stone' systems make sense of modern life, and with new awareness, we can adapt, live wiser and evolve mankind.

My analytical and logical conclusions have been deduced from 30-years of research into the primitive survival system we inherited, when our life expectancy was somewhere between 20 – 35 years*, with no hint of an intellectual brain any time soon. It becomes a problem for us today in our maturing years as we live two, three, even four times longer, stunted by a non-intellectual survival system that was designed for what is now, only the first half of our lives! I trust this is giving you a sense of huge things to come!

* I have researched the 'primitive age' question. The consensus appears to be somewhere between 20 – 35 years, median longevity, 25 – 30 years.

Why do we unconsciously repeat generational cycles?

Survival basically consists of copied behaviours handed down from one generation to the next via automatic, reactive/kneejerk subconscious repetition... mindless, robotic, learnt, observed/copied behaviours repeating generational cycles, ensuring life perpetuates itself.

The aim of this Journal is to bring survival intelligence into 21st C. Higher consciousness. **These survival programs create all kinds of problems and complications for us today when we don't understand 'The system'.**

With their much shorter lifespans, our primitive cousins:

- Did not live long enough to outgrow their hardwired survival beliefs formed in their early years.

- Remained in the 'Pack' and its 'Pack mentality' for survival reasons.

- No intellectual brain operating.

- Did not live long enough to encounter midlife problems.

- No such thing as 'The individual'.

This Journal has been written as an *introduction only* to your programmed life. For a much broader understanding, or for more specific answers to your questions, my 'Life Education' series offer greater detail and a larger portfolio of subjects from which to choose and consider.

***

Aristotle, an Ancient Greek philosopher, C 384 B.C. – 322 B.C., once said:

'Give me a child until he is seven and I will show you the man.'

What this quotation means is: The adult is living in two-time zones: fast, automatic (subliminal) subconscious *reactions* from your hardwired survival beliefs (your baggage), *are reacting from a different time zone as a present time response:*

- No thinking required.

- One reaction: two time zones.

- Generational cycles repeating themselves.

Consider this:

Would you allow a seven-year-old child to run your life? … run your business?

Of course not! but that is precisely what is happening, whether you accept or deny 'The survival system' is still hard at work today helping us survive.

***

The famous psychiatrist, Dr. Carl Jung (1875-1961) has been credited with the term 'inner child'.

How do you view the term 'inner child'? e.g., does your intellect and ego scoff at the idea? Do you think your childhood is not relevant to your age now or any age? Why? Any new thoughts?

....
....
....

I believe the term 'inner child' is one of the major reasons why our intellectual brain, without understanding 'The survival system', rejects the concept:

- denying any connection between childhood and adult time zones.

- refusing to believe that the sophisticated, worldly intelligence of the 21st C. has been upstaged by reactionary subconscious, survival intelligence.

- keeping you in denial.

- leaving you automatically and subconsciously 'stuck' in your childhood beliefs and on autopilot.

**Let's respectfully rename the 'inner child'...
your subconscious 'Backseat driver'.**

Repeating the primitive system, childhood beliefs become the foundation of our lives and with today's longer lifespan, the adult's self-fulfilling prophecies. Childhood beliefs clash with time and reality – leaving the adult feeling 'stuck' between 'what *should* happen' and 'what *is* happening!' It is the beginning of feeling confused, 'stuck' and powerless by fearful, unexpected and/or unpredictable outcomes.

***

Should I touch on anything that causes you concern, please talk with a trusted friend or counsellor. **I remind you: your confidant may be a member of the status quo! Watch for signs of resistance!**

***

HOW TO BECOME CONSCIOUS:

By becoming aware/awake/conscious to how you are *reacting* to what is happening in your life in present time, *without any intellectual input or consideration!* Your hardwired subconscious *reactions* are subliminal – you won't even notice them, but your feelings, beliefs, behaviours and attitudes are already formed, and in an instant, your subconscious reactive behaviours are on display/conscious.

***

We learn by repetition, so I have repeated the important information.

***

I have used the masculine 'he' or 'him' rather than 'he/she', 'him/her'. There is no gender bias; it simply makes for an easier read.

***

I have added a few lined pages at the end of each Section for any extra notes.

For clarity:

The child I am referring to throughout this journal is a child born some 30, 40, 50 or more years ago – not today's child.

Let's make sense of 'The system', transcend your childhood baggage, liberate your life and your maturing needs.

SECTION 1:

THE EVOLUTIONARY SECRETS OF LIFE

1. Your personal development assessment..........................1

2. The Evolving Secrets of Life – Struggling?
Feeling underpowered? Here's why!..............................3

3. Liberating You and the 21st Century from
primitive survival intelligence..6

1. YOUR PERSONAL DEVELOPMENT ASSESSMENT:

The following questions have been designed to give you an understanding of how the primitive *reactive* survival programs are directing your life today:

1. On a scale from 1 – 10, 10 being the highest, how much do you 'Need to belong'? Reasons?
   ....
   ....
   ....

2. Do you conform with the 'Pack' aka the status quo and its 'one rule fits all' mentality? Do you fear abandonment or rejection if you choose independence above fitting in? Do you know why?
   ....
   ....
   ....

3. Do you acknowledge and work with your feelings, instincts and senses? Are you aware of their significance?
   ....
   ....
   ....

4. Do you fear moving out of your comfort zones? Do you fear change? Self-expression? Independence? Standing in the spotlight? Do you know why?
   ....
   ....
   ....

5. Are you aware of any childhood beliefs, behaviours or attitudes?
   ....
   ....
   ....

If not, then without conscious thought, your reactions to what is happening in your adult life have been subconscious reactions directing your life from a different time zone. The two time zones in action. Can you think of an example?
   ....
   ....
   ....

6. How are your stress levels today? Where are you on a scale of 1 – 10, 10 being the most stressed? Did you know our 'fight or flight' adrenal reactions are a primitive reaction? They *cannot* discriminate between fear and modern-day stress. Adrenal fatigue... primitive body; 21st C.
   ....
   ....
   ....

Let's check your answers from 1 to 6, against 'The survival system'.

2. THE EVOLVING SECRETS OF LIFE – STRUGGLING? FEELING UNDERPOWERED? HERE'S WHY!

Guess how many primitive survival programs have been switched off? None!

Compare each of your Personal Development Assessment answers to our survival programming:

1. The primal will to survive translated into our 'Need to belong'.

2. The 'Pack' and its 'Pack' mentality, maintained order and helped the tribe survive.

3. We were born self-protective with feelings, instincts and senses.

4. Fear was built into our DNA, helping us survive and live within its safe, self-protective boundaries.

5. The subconscious mind was our primitive memory with its fast, automatic 'keeping you safe' reactions. Reactive behaviours aided our survival.

6. 'Fight or flight' reactions to fear helped us escape danger and survive!

***

7. Hormonal changes in adolescence/early teens.

8. Sexual/primal urges to perpetuate the survival of *all* species.

9. The predictable breakdown of our physical selves as we age.

Simple, robotic, reactive, repetitive = SURVIVAL. No thinking required!

"Give me a child until he is seven and I will show you the man." Aristotle.

ONE RESPONSE – TWO TIME ZONES – SUBCONSCIOUS 'AUTOPILOT'.

What we see repeatedly as little kids we deem to be 'normal', and the way life works… forever. Those beliefs and behaviours are hardwired into our reactive subconscious memory and become the structural foundations for potentially, the whole of our lives.

SUMMARISING:

When the survival system was created, our primitive cousins did not live long enough to encounter midlife problems; we had no intellectual brain and 'The individual' had not evolved!

It becomes a problem for us today as we mature:

- unconsciously reacting subconsciously

- automatically 'stuck' in two time zones

- unconsciously living in our childhood hardwired belief system and fear-based comfort zones

- a survival 'need to belong' that naturally conforms with the status quo and its 'Pack mentality'.

THESE ARE THE EVOLUTIONARY SECRETS OF LIFE.

Any thoughts?

....
....
....
....
....
....
....
....

3. LIBERATING YOU AND THE 21ST CENTURY FROM 'REACTIVE' PRIMITIVE SURVIVAL INTELLIGENCE

Today, as we live a much longer lifespan, hardwired reactive subconscious survival beliefs from the first seven years, become the maturing adult's unconscious baggage. No wonder we feel 'stuck' and confused, seeking therapy in midlife!

This is where it gets really interesting.

Self-protective denial:

Still in primitive survival mode today, anything deemed confronting and/or interfering with your hardwired childhood survival beliefs will be blocked by an automatic subconscious denial reaction.

The good news: when you realise you are automatically *reacting* without thinking, you can choose to override denial and create new, intellectually empowering outcomes with unlimited choices that can expand your life exponentially.

The two time zones. Questions to ponder:

I believe most people leave their childhood not liking themselves. How could we like ourselves with so many conforming controls and standards to live up to, dependence issues and without a powerful ID? With this in mind:

What's holding you back today? e.g., thoughts of 'not enough'? Self-doubts? Fear of abandonment/rejection?

....
....
....

What coping behaviours do you use? e.g., blaming, avoidance? Any others?
....
....
....

Note any negative remarks or words from childhood or your teen years that still affect you today:
....
....
....

Any truth to them or do they automatically appear when you think about yourself? Have you updated your adult self-image recently?
....
....
....

Again, these are the two time zones. Those beliefs and automatic behaviours and reactions are *not* who you are today. Your powerful catalyst for change is to like the adult version of yourself. Time to transcend 'The system' that is 'dumbing us down' and stunting our potential today… time to add some delightful realism!

Notes:

SECTION 2:

BECOMING CONSCIOUS

4. Why debriefing your childhood is key to adult consciousness..13

5. The blueprint for life – The childhood model..............15

6. Benefits to living in your childhood model..................18

7. Connecting with your emotional life..........................21

8. An understanding of the subconscious mind and survival..23

4. WHY DEBRIEFING YOUR CHILDHOOD IS KEY TO ADULT CONSCIOUSNESS

The military and businesses have debriefings, don't they?

Did you know there are courses to help deinstitutionalise people who have been living and/or working within regulated structures over a long period of time?

Why not a childhood debriefing?

Childhood is, after all, the most structured and regulated time in our lives.

On what do we base our lives if not our childhood?

- Where do our feelings about ourselves and 'not enough' come from?

- Where do our beliefs, comfort zones, behaviours etc. originate?

- Where do our fears come from? e.g., fear of change.

- Where else but childhood, did we learn to fit in and conform?

Without a childhood debriefing, how do we build a dream-team Higher consciousness with our inner child aka our subconscious 'Backseat driver'? How do we connect to the reactive survival system we were born into and the *Gargantuan realisation* that you, me, all of us, are living in Aristotle's two time zones?

Haven't we all experienced times in our adult lives when we have:

- Felt 'not enough'?

- Trusted naively?

- Felt pressure to conform?

- Used avoidance and blame as a way of coping?

- Remained silent, not willing to question authority, risk embarrassment, rejection, criticism or judgement?

- Felt frustrated, 'stuck' and powerless?

- Heard ourselves repeat something to our kids we heard in our childhood?

- Saw our mother's eyes in an unexpected reflection?

What we don't acknowledge, directs our lives!

DENIAL THAT THE 21ST CENTURY IS BEING UPSTAGED BY A PRIMITIVE REACTIVE SUBCONSCIOUS SURVIVAL SYSTEM, IS OUR GREATEST ADVERSARY TO AN EMPOWERED, LIBERATED AND EVOLVING LIFE.

5. THE BLUEPRINT FOR LIFE – THE CHILDHOOD MODEL

The literal childhood model of life is formed in the first seven years.

Did you know you have a childhood model? that your children are establishing their childhood model? and your grandchildren will assemble their childhood model? No? It was news to me too. Debriefing the contents is one of the most empowering and liberating experiences of our maturing lives.

What can we expect to find in our childhood 'model of life':

- Generational themes, values and attitudes.

- A 'need to belong' – to survive.

- Everything we observed, heard and felt repeatedly.

- Coping and copied behaviours such as staying out of the spotlight.

- A need to fit in and conform.

- Fear and comfort zone boundaries.

- Little reference to time or change.

- Standards, controls and limitations.

- Should, should not, must and supposed to beliefs.

- No responsibility for ourselves.

- No alternative choices – we lived in a yes-or-no, either/or world.

- Feelings of powerlessness.

- No sign of independence.

- A serious, personal world with no humour about ourselves.

- Resentments, anger, regrets lists.

- Images and beliefs about ourselves that were formed from the opinions and feedback from outside sources.

Any others?
....
....
....

As a literal little kid, we believed everything at trusting face-value. Even though there is no factual data to back up our literal childhood beliefs, those hardwired judgements live deep within our reactive subconscious mind, creating enormous self-doubt, trapping us in a tiny world of fear and self-protective behaviours. Those beliefs, unless intercepted, potentially become our forever subconscious 'Backseat driver'.

When you were young, you didn't know or understand that:

- fear

- your 'need to belong' and

- Emotional dependence on 'the group'

had the power to usurp your individual and maturing development.

Living in childhood model constraints will always leave the adult with feelings of self-doubt, 'not enough', compromised and powerless.

Give yourself a break! Your inner child got it wrong about you, my inner child got it wrong about me, everyone's inner child gets it wrong… how could they not?

From the childhood model list above, which areas in your life will need reviewing and/or updating?
....
....
....

How are your should, should not, have to and supposed to beliefs, learnt in childhood, impacting your life today? Any you can update or release?
....
....
....

Viewing your childhood as a temporary learning experience, rather than allowing it to remain unconscious, unacknowledged and permanent, introduces a powerful new perspective to the adult position and huge possibilities for our future potential.

***

Did you know… there are benefits to living in your childhood model?

6. BENEFITS TO LIVING IN YOUR CHILDHOOD MODEL

First, there is no self-responsibility in the childhood model. Your carers were responsible for you in every way. You were learning the basics e.g., brushing your teeth twice each day and combing your hair. You may have been 'responsible' for one or more of your siblings, but the little kid in you couldn't make the distinction between responsibility for others and responsibility for himself.

Did anyone tell you that you needed to update your childhood belief system? No? It was news to me too! No wonder we feel 'stuck' and powerless as we mature. Let's change that, shall we?

Do you blame? Is blaming your way of coping with life? Does blaming make you feel more or less empowered? Can you give an example?
....
....
....

Do you avoid? (My favourite). Avoidance has become such a popular way of coping with life that this behaviour has given birth to the term, 'Avoidant personality'. Do you pretend to yourself that everything is okay or that it will be okay? Do you tell yourself that it doesn't really matter? Does this let you off the hook or does it leave you waiting for the axe to fall?
....
....
....

Do you use rebellion, procrastination, passive/aggressive behaviours as a way of coping? Can you give an example?
....
....
....

Do you stay out of the spotlight? Do you choose not to speak up... even on matters important to you? Any examples? (Unfortunately, when you don't speak up, people think you agree with them.)
....
....
....

Any other coping behaviours/strategies?
....
....
....

SUMMARISING:

You, the adult, are *not* powerless. But, coming from your *reactive* subconscious 'Backseat driver' and its unconscious 'model of life', you *feel* powerless!

Today, you have no such boundaries. You are:

- physically independent

- able to use your evolving brain to give you an intellectual edge over your childhood model *literal* belief system.

It's your 'Backseat driver' living in its fear-based comfort zones and its tiny, powerless, serious, personal world, with its automatic subconscious reactions to what is happening in current time... that is blocking the unaware adult from owning his potential and a much more 'lived-in' life.

How will your new awareness potentially change and empower your life? How do you feel?
....
....
....

Many more examples of the two time zones in action will be investigated in Section III.

Now let's find out how to access our emotional life. Feelings are the individual's unique power base.

7. CONNECTING WITH YOUR EMOTIONAL LIFE

Over the vastness of time, our feelings have been demoted in order of importance behind our intellect. I believe most of us are out of touch with our feelings, not realising their significance and their self-protective survival power. Your feelings are unique and personal to you and play a major role in creating 'the individual' in all of us.

Your feelings are your constant companions – guiding, alerting and intuiting you – making you aware of your connection with yourself, others, the outside world and your position within those spheres. Feelings want your support, recognition and acknowledgement for all the work they do. *Fair enough too!*

Note: you are not your feelings. Feelings are fleeting and create the emotion you are experiencing.

How do you access your feelings?

Asking yourself regularly, *'What am I feeling?'* is bringing your attention back to yourself, aware of the many changes in your emotional connection with yourself. Recognising and acknowledging your current emotional state is a major shift in your personal power.

Initially, don't be surprised if you don't know what you are feeling. With practise, you will quickly recognise your feelings as you align with their emotional intelligence aka your survival intelligence.

What am I feeling?

Think of this as a guessing game. Ask yourself, *'What am I feeling?'*
....
....
....

Continue asking yourself. When you have guessed correctly, you will feel moved; you will soften or resonate with that acknowledged feeling, aware of how you are coping in your present situation.

Intense feelings:

When you recognise and acknowledge intense feelings such as anger, simple acknowledgement such as:

'I'm furious!', 'I'm angry', 'I am so-o-o cheesed off!' said with equal intensity,

will pacify the emotional intensity. Use expletives, yell, whatever works for you. You may have to acknowledge the feeling several times, depending on its intensity. The aim is to soften your intense feelings and their frustration, so you are in control.

Feelings are one of the most powerful and often undervalued powerbases in our lives today. Making sense? Any thoughts? How/what are you feeling?
....
....
....

To complete this section, let's take a closer look at the subconscious mind and its part in our survival history.

8. AN UNDERSTANDING OF THE SUBCONSCIOUS MIND AND SURVIVAL

Although there are many books available on how to work with the subconscious mind, I now wish to add more understanding of its importance in our lives from a *survival reactive perspective* and how it relates to our lives today.

Did you know?

- The subconscious mind is pro-life and has been helping us survive since the beginning of time.

- The subconscious mind was our survival memory before our intellectual brain evolved.

- **The subconscious is still our survival memory in the first seven years of every child's life, before our intellectual brain takes over!**

- The subconscious mind does not recognise or respond to the intellect… no matter our age!

- Your subconscious mind lives in its own time zone i.e., it does not live by man's manufactured time. There are no clocks or watches in its world.

- The subconscious mind does not conform to man's rules.

- Your subconscious is always on alert… ready to work for you.

Your subconscious mind has been compared to a six-year-old child:

- It cannot reason, question, discriminate or make distinctions.

- It lives in its literal world, believing everything you say, trusting you and your words, especially those spoken with emotional intensity – be careful what you say and what you wish for.

- It loves repetition and images.

When you think of your subconscious mind, think of a literal, serious, 'personal' six-year-old child living in its own time zone.

How to work with your subconscious mind today is covered in Section V: The big picture.

Before we go deeper, let's make the distinction between a subconscious reaction and a memory:

Subconscious reactions are fast, automatic, subliminal reactions directing you to believe, feel or act in a particular way to your present situation.

Memories are reminders of something from your past that are not directing you to do anything. They are usually attached to your senses e.g., the smell of a roast dinner cooking taking you back to childhood family gatherings, a song reminding you of someone special or reminiscing about a joyful event etc.

Notes:

SECTION 3:

EXAMPLES OF THE TWO TIME ZONES IN YOUR LIFE

9. Time zone differences 31

10. The 'Need to belong' – *an innate force* 34

11. Your 'Need to belong' and *the status quo today* 37

12. Choices 39

13. Conformity 41

14. Time and change 43

15. The 'personal' serious world of a child 45

16. Fear 47

17. Emotional dependence 49

18. Perfection 51

19. All you need is love 53

9. TIME ZONE DIFFERENCES

Let's separate the time zones of our lives and add further explanation:

- Your subconscious 'Backseat driver' and its model of life remained in the childhood time zone forever.

- You continued to develop physically until around 21 years of age.

- Your intellectual brain continued its development until approximately 25 years of age.

- Around seven-years-old, your emotional life was demoted in order of importance behind your intellectual brain.

***

To progress in midlife:

- Your emotional life, the feminine right side of your brain wants to catch up with her now fully developed physical and evolving intellectual counterparts to complete the Yin/Yang balance of life.

***

- Your emotional life is the backbone of your life.

- Emotional expansion, emotional expression and emotional independence are the *Acts of courage*.

- Your IQ cannot expand your courage.

- She is your courage; he is your intellect.

More on midlife and the power of reconnecting with your emotional life later.

FOREWORD

We can never cut/severe the cords to our hardwired subconscious *survival beliefs*, the beliefs formed in the first seven years, but we can disarm their 'live' power with our new awareness.

This is how our adult intellect can build a 'dream-team' Higher consciousness with our subconscious 'Backseat driver' and transcend feelings of 'stuckness' and powerlessness.

When you understand the *'reactive* survival system' we were born into, we, as a global community, will evolve – especially aware of our immense parenting power in the first seven years of every child's life.

10. THE 'NEED TO BELONG' – *AN INNATE FORCE*

Belonging to the 'Pack' kept us safe and protected and was the caveman's way of surviving. 'The system' hasn't changed!

Our innate 'Need to belong' and emotional dependence on 'The group' in the first half of our lives, becomes an unconscious intimidating force, often conflicting with our maturing needs. *'Ah-ha'!*

Let's find out how this new understanding fits in with our lives today:

Childhood years:

In a nutshell, our very survival depends on someone caring for us, doesn't it? Our primal will to survive translates into a 'Need to belong', to be loved and cared for. Abandonment is a primal fear.

Teenage years:

Teens shift alliances from the tribal family to their generation. Not fitting in, exclusion, rejection or non-acceptance from their peer group is dangerous territory for teens. That's how important a sense of belonging and its emotional support is, in the first half of our lives.

The unaware/reactive adult:

This adult feels confused and 'stuck'. He wants a bigger life, but he doesn't understand 'The system'. Fear, his need to belong and dependence on others for emotional support prevents him from acting independently. Feelings of 'stuckness' is one of the first signs that his emotional life is ready to expand and support him.

Empowered concepts:

The maturing adult acknowledges his yearning for independence. He understands the two time zones and realises he no longer 'needs to belong' for childhood survival or for his teenage generation's support and acceptance. Emotional dependence on others interferes with his maturing position and belongs to the past. Acknowledgement of his liberated and empowered position; that he is now a separate and complete entity, allows him to make emotionally independent choices to progress his life... if he has the courage.

Is your innate 'need to belong' interfering with your maturing needs? Can you give examples? Note how you feel.
....
....
....

Are you okay spending time alone or do you constantly seek company? Any reasons?
....
....
....

Has your tribal family accepted your maturing position, or do they expect you to fall in line like you did when you were a child? Do you find yourself making excuses not to attend family functions?
....
....
....

Do you feel pressure to conform with your generation's expectations? Is fear of rejection by your peer group intimidating you? If yes, how?

....
....
....

11. YOUR 'NEED TO BELONG' AND *THE STATUS QUO TODAY*

Let's find out how your childhood and teenage 'Need to belong' for survival and acceptance respectively, work against the maturing individual's desire for emotional independence today.

The unaware adult:

The unconscious adult has little understanding of his innate need to belong. Fear of rejection, fear of self-expression and criticism or judgement from 'the group' and its 'Pack' mentality keep him in his childhood fear-based comfort zone, emotionally contracted, not living up to his potential for fear of upsetting family, friends, neighbours and relationships' wider social circles.

Empowered concepts:

Today, the aware adult rationalises that he no longer needs to belong for survival or acceptance. It is his duty of care to himself and his maturing right to make independent choices above the need to belong and its conformity issues; *seeking his own approval, not just above peer group approval, but above status quo approval per se!* Huge!

How much is fear of abandonment and/or fear of rejection determining the size of your life? What would you like to change?
....
....
....

Is fear keeping you emotionally contracted/stunted? What are you *not* doing for fear of upsetting the people around you? Are you less stressed by not acting? Or are you adding to your anger, resentments and regrets lists?

....
....
....

In comparison, can you think of an example when you stood in the spotlight and put your position forward? How did you feel?

....
....
....

It's as simple as it is complicated, isn't it?

12. CHOICES:

Do you believe you have choices?

The literal child and choices:

The literal, powerless, dependent, security conscious child has no understanding of choices. He lives in a black-or-white, either/or world of right-or-wrong, can-or-can't, yes-or-no.

The unaware adult:

Feeling 'stuck' in a world that superficially appears to have no alternative choices, is a difficult and frustrating fit for the unaware maturing adult. This inflexible reactive black-or-white mindset further impacts his fear of making the wrong decision and/or stepping outside his fear-based childhood comfort zones. A black-or-white mindset may also indicate to the casual observer, especially in business, that this adult has not evolved in his personal development. A fixed, inflexible mindset is difficult for everyone to work with, not just for this individual.

Empowered concepts:

The aware adult rationalises that his life can be summed up by choices made by himself or someone else. Choices are at the heart of individual freedom. Grey areas of negotiation and conciliation and alternative choices give him lots of wriggle room and incredible power to express himself and to expand his emotional freedom exponentially. There is no going back to the suffocating either/or black-or-white world of his 'Backseat driver'.

Have you been taught that choices made in your best interests are selfish? What are your thoughts now?
....
....
....

Do you procrastinate? Does the fear of making a wrong decision freeze your decision making? Great question. Can you give an example. What could you do differently? Baby steps?
....
....
....

Have you ever negotiated a win-win for all parties? How did you feel? Are you now willing to take the next step?
....
....
....

13. CONFORMITY:

We have a love/hate relationship with conformity, don't we? It's a double-edged sword. We feel safe living in the fold, but at the same time, it's stunting our potential. Let's dig deeper:

The literal child and conformity:

The literal, powerless, dependent, security conscious child has no understanding of conformity. You, me and all the other little kids were programmed to conform. Learnt behaviours such as 'follow the leader', the concept of safety in numbers and fitting in were part of our upbringing, basically to maintain 'order'. Fair enough too, but this doesn't allow a child to feel like an individual. *Is this where we got the idea that we didn't fit in anywhere?*

The unaware adult:

This adult doesn't understand that fear, his childhood beliefs, dependence on peer group acceptance and its 'Pack' mentality, are all contributing to his feelings of 'stuckness', frustration and powerlessness. He even squashes his maturing needs and his potential, for fear of upsetting family, friends and wider social circles, adding to the chip on his shoulder. *Conformity sucks the power from this individual.*

Empowered concepts:

The maturing adult is aware of tribal, generational and societal conformity conditioning and expectations. He also acknowledges and respects his emotional maturing needs. *He reasons that he is not rebelling against his generation or the status quo, but rather, choosing to make independent decisions that work in his best interests today.* He is transcending his fear of rejection, while acknowledging deeper survival and acceptance issues that will open his world exponentially – the awakened adult's rite of passage.

What beliefs do you have about conformity?
....
....
....

Are you intimidated by the thought of your peer group's reaction if you choose a different path to their expectations?
....
....
....

How big could your life be without conformity issues? With a little bit of courage, what's the first thing you could change to own your power? *A delightful question!* ☺
....
....
....

14. TIME AND CHANGE

Let's find out how the effects of time and change impact us today:

The literal child – time and change:

The literal, powerless, dependent, security conscious child had no understanding of time and change. He lived in a 'now' world. Change is scary to a child. The little kid in you wants everything to stay the same. Fearful 'what if's' such as *'what if I fail'*, or *'what if everyone laughs at me'* intimidate him, keeping him safe and secure in his comfort zone and scared of change.

The unaware adult:

This adult has trouble accepting change of any kind. He wants 'what *is* happening' to be what his beliefs say, *'should* be happening'. This individual doesn't understand why he feels so fearful and just like his 'Backseat driver', usually retreats, unwilling to expand his comfort zones. *It's easy to see from his behaviours that this character is stuck in time, isn't it?*

Empowered concepts:

The aware, maturing adult is conscious of the two time zones operating in his life and understands where his fear of change is coming from. He accepts that his life is less about control and more about flexibility and that he is a 'work in progress'. Inner preparedness for the inevitability of change is enormously powerful. Personal power and free will are in the hands of this individual who is on the same frequency as the Universe's forward flow of life.

Has time and change been affecting and disempowering you and/or your business? What are some of your new options?
....
....
....

How are childhood fear-based *'what if's'* impacting you today?
....
....
....

Does fear of embarrassing yourself hold you back if you don't succeed the first time? With this new perspective, can you see 'trying' differently?
....
....
....

Now you understand this concept... what's your next step?
....
....
....

Don't you just love this? Seeing how your childhood beliefs/reactions interfere with your adult time zone puts everything into perspective, doesn't it?

15. THE 'PERSONAL' SERIOUS WORLD OF A CHILD

We often hear the words, 'it's not personal', don't we? Let's dig deeper…

The literal child and personal:

The literal, powerless, dependent, security conscious child had no understanding of 'personal'. He is totally reliant upon others for everything in his tiny, serious, personal world and from this perspective, life always revolved around him. Adding to his seriousness, he has no humour about himself! He will laugh at other kids falling over, for example, but not when he falls over. If something isn't working out, he blames himself – it's always his fault… even divorce. **Life is always serious and personal to the little kid in you.** ☹ *Beautiful!*

The unaware adult:

The unaware adult doesn't understand that taking remarks, situations and life personally has him on the back foot thinking powerlessly and/or behaving like a child. Everything is scary to the 'personal' personality as he clings to his defensive positions. He becomes difficult to work with and eventually may be seen as precious. It's a very tiny and scary place for him too.

Empowered concepts:

The maturing aware adult realises that removing 'personal' from his life, especially when dealing with others, softens and opens his world exponentially. He has loosened up, taken the seriousness out of most situations, can see humour in himself and his predicaments. **He is powerfully aware that his automatic subconscious reactions from childhood are keeping him in his backseat** driver's tiny, 'personal', self-protective and emotionally stunted world. More power to this aware adult.

How has 'personal' been disempowering your adult life? Any examples?
....
....
....

How much bigger could your life be without 'personal' interfering? What can you change immediately?
....
....
....

Does lack of humour about yourself and your life disempower you today? What can you change to feel more light-hearted?
....
....
....

16. FEAR

Fear was/is part of our basic survival DNA. Fear warned us of imminent physical danger when we lived in a hostile environment with a much shorter lifespan. Our adrenals responded to fear with 'fight or flight' *reactions* – exactly as they do today, making us stronger and faster to escape physical danger. Fear's job has always been to keep us safe; it still is an extremely good warning system.

Let's find out how, why, when and where fear is coming from today.

The literal child and fear:

Fear was your childhood survival companion. Fear is your 'Backseat driver's' comfort zone dictator. Every child instinctively obeys fear, or he might get into trouble. Every time fear was present, the little kid in you retreated. The child's intellectual brain is in its rudimentary stages and cannot distinguish between a real and/or a perceived fear.

The unaware adult:

The unaware reactive adult is unlikely to go against his fear-based childhood comfort zones. He continues to be managed and limited by fear and its intimidatory survival tactics. This adult doesn't understand where his fear is coming from. His emotional life remains on hold as he continues to live frustratingly under his potential. Without an intellectual understanding of fear and its role in our survival, anxiousness and 'settling' become a way of life for this individual.

Empowered concepts:

The empowered adult realises that most of his fears are perceived fears from childhood – the 'what if' variety. He also realises that when he expands his childhood comfort zones, or when he moves into unknown territory, he will automatically feel anxious and fearful. Understanding this, the empowered adult can progress, with fear accompanying him... as it should, no longer his Master.

One more thing: *most of us want to feel safe and secure, not just in childhood but throughout our lives, which is another reason why fear is so intimidating.*

What are your tell-tale signs that fear is present? Where do you physically feel fear? E.g., your solar plexus?
....
....
....

What were you thinking immediately before fear presented itself? Remember: every reaction is pre-empted by a thought.
....
....
....

What circumstances push your fear buttons?
....
....
....

Did you know, fear loves surprises? It's in its element when you are surprised by an unexpected outcome. *It really is a menace, isn't it?* ☺

17. EMOTIONAL DEPENDENCE

We never really think about the issues arising from our emotional dependence on important others, do we? It's a big one… let's investigate:

The literal child and emotional dependence:

The need to belong and emotional dependence on the tribal family for survival is a basic requirement for every child. Knowing that our carers love us and support us, the child feels understood, affirming that he is okay. *Love this!*

The unaware adult:

The unaware adult has not reconciled that his need to belong, emotional dependence on his tribal family and a need for his generation's acceptance keeps him fitting in and conforming, adding to his feelings of frustration and powerlessness. He finds it difficult to stand up, to say what he wants or needs, and he doesn't understand why he feels 'stuck', caught between his emotional dependence on others for support and his desire for independence. *'Ah-ha!'*

Empowered concepts:

This adult understands the two time zones and now intercepts childhood beliefs that are not working for him today. He adjusts his coping behaviours to fit his maturing stage of life, becomes aware of his patterns, and reviews and updates his self-image. **He is no longer reliant on others for emotional support and to feel okay about himself.** **He can lean on himself and endorse his own approval!** *Huge!*

How will this new understanding of emotional dependence change your life?

....
....
....

18. PERFECTION

Let's find out where the idealistic 'need to be perfect' has its origins:

The literal child and perfection:

The little kid in you tried its hardest to keep up, to fit in, to get things right and to be good. It's an unconscious bargaining/ reciprocal arrangement to please your carers and important others... in return, you will be cared for and loved, and your carers will be proud of you. The security conscious child and his unrealistic/ idealistic expectations of himself may eventually believe he has to be perfect to be loved and accepted! *'Ah-ha!'*

The unaware adult:

This adult has no understanding of the connection between childhood and present time. The unconscious childhood 'need for perfection' is a massive burden for the unaware adult, controlling his every move. He feels like he's walking on a tight rope and never feels the freedom to try something new in case he fails and can't live up to his imaginary childhood ideal and image of perfection.

The empowered adult:

The empowered adult has realised that the need for perfection is a child's unrealistic and idealistic expectation. By releasing the straitjacket effect of his childhood idealism, he feels relaxed enough to challenge himself and his current circumstances and make choices that work in his best interests, perfect or not.

Have you felt the straitjacket effect of needing to be perfect? How did it impact you? How will this new understanding change your life?

....
....
....

19. ALL YOU NEED IS LOVE

John Lennon wrote the lyrics. The Beatles sang "All you need is love" making the words famous in 1967. The gist was needing love from others.

Let's find out how *all you need is love* relates to the whole of our lives when we add the two time zones:

The literal child and love:

Coming from the literal child's perspective, 'all you need is love' means needing love from his family and friends to be cared for and supported.

The unaware adult:

The unaware adult, who has not expanded the broader meaning of love, will continue to think that *he needs love from others to feel okay about himself.* This childhood model survival belief is so powerful, that it not only leaves the naïve adult stuck in his dependence on others, but it also leaves him vulnerable and easily played by the unconscionable among us; not daring to think independently, always feeling the pressure to fit in with the status quo mindset even if he doesn't agree! without understanding why and the bigger picture.

Empowered concepts:

This maturing adult has progressed to a more worldly view of love. He realises that self-love and self-acceptance gives him positive vibes about himself and powerful independent choices... that he is okay – *with or without others' approval.* He rationalises his need to balance his social and maturing personal needs, ultimately making choices that work in his best interests.

How will self-love change your image and present circumstances?
....
....
....

If the above ten examples have piqued your curiosity, 31 examples of the two time zones are presented in 'You and your inner child today' Journal. They have been written from a child's understanding of a particular subject, contrasted by an empowered adult perspective, with an affirmation taking the child and adult into their Higher consciousness 'dream-team' future together. For more information, please check my website: louiselkallaway.com

Notes:

SECTION 4:

UPDATING AND LIBERATING YOUR CHILDHOOD IMAGE

20. Your identity 59

21. Liking yourself today 62

22. Why liking yourself is the catalyst for change 65

20. YOUR IDENTITY

Let's update your ID.

The literal child and your identity:

Your beliefs about yourself, your self-esteem, sense of importance and self-worth aka your identity, were all formed from the feedback you received and perceived from your carers and other external sources. Feedback was confirmed on an instinctual and emotional level by how others *reacted* to you. The literal child is unable to question, reason or discriminate.

The unaware adult:

The unaware maturing adult continues to allow the opinions of others from a different time zone to validate his feelings about himself and his identity, creating more self-doubt and adding more fuel to not liking himself. Remaining in his 'Backseat driver's' image, he feels 'less than', his self-doubts impacting his willingness to go after what he wants with any degree of confidence.

Empowered concepts:

The awakening adult is working with his new and empowered self-image, acknowledging his many talents, qualifications, life education, experiences and wisdom today. He is no longer stunted by outdated, 'were they ever real' beliefs. He admits he is okay! and is now a work in progress and loving it!

Do you remember any words or phrases from childhood that hurt you or defined you? You may like to check your previous answers from page 7 or add a defining moment here.
....
....
....

Has your childhood image, and/or your feelings and beliefs held you back? Any examples?
....
....
....

No more 'not enough', 'not good enough' and self-doubts sabotaging your dreams before you've even started!

What you were told as a child and any random comments thrown at you as a teenager, is *not* who you are today! Let's build you an updated, empowering self-image with all your achievements etc.

Take your time. I want you to *feel the difference* between the time zones! Think about who you are today – your education and/or life education, experiences, any issues you have overcome, how proud you felt of yourself etc. Use inspiring adjectives to get you started on your new image; choose words or phrases you resonate with and/or *empowering words and phrases you can grow into*. Be courageous! Who do you want to be? What would this feel like/look like to you? How much difference will a new self-image make to your life moving forward? This is

a grand opportunity to change childhood dislike of yourself into an upbeat 'rave review' about you and your future possibilities. Have fun creating your new self-image:

....
....
....
....
....
....
....
....
....
....
....
....
....
....
....
....
....
....
....
....
....
....
....
....
....
....
....
....

You are a work-in-progress. Continue to update your image from time to time as you become more valuable to yourself first, and then others.

21. LIKING YOURSELF TODAY

I believe most of us don't think too much about the crossover between childhood and adult time zones, and what that really means. Our age and time simply move us forward.

I also believe that most people leave their childhood not liking themselves. As mentioned earlier, how could we like ourselves with all those controls, standards, dependence issues and without a powerful ID?

Liking yourself is a breakthrough and the catalyst for change, leading to feelings of inner security, trust, confidence and belief in yourself. The relationship you have with yourself sets the tone for all areas of your life. When you feel a genuine liking for yourself, you will give yourself more consideration and change will be based on your Higher conscious needs.

How do you start the journey and transition into liking who you are today?

There is usually a catalyst or a motivator. It's always personal. What's been happening in your life lately:

Have you been feeling 'stuck', overwhelmed, even defeated? Defeat manifests as a sense of hopelessness resulting in inactivity.

....
....
....
....
....
....
....
....

Do you feel you must always be accepted, like you did as a teen? Can you think of any examples?
....
....
....

Do you wonder if you'll be able to handle the next situation, the next set of circumstances? How does self-doubt creep into your life?
....
....
....

Do you worry if you can't live up to others' expectations of you? How is this impacting you?
....
....
....

Do you feel there is something missing from your life? Can you name it? Can you explain your feeling?
....
....
....

Have you had a huge disappointment recently; loss of a job, a dream, a love affair that hasn't worked out for you? How has this impacted you?
....
....
....

Have you *not* been feeling well lately – physically, emotionally, mentally? What impact is this having on you?

....
....
....

Are you depressed? (Depression is anger turned inwards. There is no loudness or aggression, but rather a quiet, all-embracing feeling of despondency). Why are you so angry with yourself?

....
....
....

To understand your move into Higher consciousness, you need to acknowledge your motivator or catalyst to disconnect its power. The act of giving anything power over you today, belongs to the past.

This is also about you disconnecting from the first half of your life's rules, dependence, conditioning, childhood dislike of yourself, any defining moments, feelings of overwhelm etc., as you move forward.

What is your motivator or catalyst for change? How is it impacting you and your feelings? Go deep and wide. Give it the full scope of your understanding:

....
....
....
....
....
....
....
....
....

22. WHY LIKING YOURSELF IS THE CATALYST FOR CHANGE

When you change your attitude towards yourself with self-love and self-approval and you update your self-image, your Higher conscious needs will allow life-changing possibilities, such as:

- Becoming more courageous.

- No longer allowing others to be more important than you.

- Living up to the promises you make to yourself.

- A new sense of inner security with no strings to the outside world.

- Less intimidated by fear, current circumstances, those in authority or stronger personalities.

- Speaking up on matters that are important to you.

- Willing to explore and work with your nature, talents, strengths and potential. Maybe consult with a professional talented in any areas you classify as your weakness.

- Recognising and working with your new choices.

- Allowing your personal power and free will to forge an independent, more 'lived-in' life... *love that!*

Based on a genuine liking for yourself, what changes would you like to make? Short term and long term?

Notes:

SECTION 5:

THE BIG PICTURE – BE INSPIRED… BECOME INSPIRING

23. How to work with your
    subconscious mind today 73

24. The status quo and 'The system'
    vs personal power.. 76

25. What is personal power? 80

26. Reinterpreting the 'Midlife Crisis' 81

27. The 'individual' and its place in history..................... 87

A tribute to your inner child

23. HOW TO WORK WITH YOUR SUBCONSCIOUS MIND TODAY:

Following on from 'An understanding of the subconscious mind and survival' in Section II, let's find out how to work with your subconscious mind today:

What does the subconscious love to work with?

- repetition

- images

- passion and emotional intensity.

How are you contributing to your current situation?

When your subconscious hears you say repeatedly with passion and emotional intensity, things like:

- 'I'm always experiencing delays!' or

- 'I can never have what I want!' or

- 'I'm always in debt!'

Guess what? You will get more of the same. Your subconscious believes that is what you want! It's literal! It takes you at your word!

How to work with and benefit from your subconscious:

- Become aware of your internal monologue.

- Use positive, simple words that cannot be misinterpreted – remember, your subconscious can be likened to a six-year-old child.

- Use short direct sentences/statements.

- Speak and feel with emotional intensity.

- *Speak in present time… as if you already have what you want.*

- Visualise images of yourself with the item you are seeking.

- Concentrate on one item at a time.

- Repeat your statement over and over every day – especially first thing in the morning and before you go to sleep.

- Continue repeating your statement, until you get what you want.

Be sincere. You can't trick kids on an emotional level, that's their language, and the language of your subconscious mind.

Don't decide how you think it should happen – your subconscious doesn't work with the intellect, rules, beliefs or traditional thinking. Watch out for the unexpected.

Don't decide how long it should take – your subconscious has no clocks or watches in its world.

Decide what it is you are seeking or wanting to change. Construct your short, passionate simple statement using the above format.

……………………………………………………………………………………
……………………………………………………………………………………
……………………………………………………………………………………

Your request is now out of your hands and your learnt controlling behaviour. Stay alert for clues. Be patient and keep the faith. Know your subconscious is devoted to you and is doing everything in its power to deliver your wish. Let your subconscious do its job. Persistence and dedication wins!

24. THE STATUS QUO AND 'THE SYSTEM' VS PERSONAL POWER

Let's detail how and why the *'two against one'* system works against the maturing adult, his personal power and free will.

Primitive survival:

Our survival depended on belonging to 'The Pack'. Living in a hostile environment, 'The Pack' provided shelter and a sense of safety. Leaving the Pack was *never* a consideration!

Today:

As well as our survival programming, we have an evolving intellectual brain, a much longer lifespan and 'The individual' has come of age.

Conformity is high on Society's agenda to maintain discipline and order, but who says adults must continue to live under the rules and conditioning we learnt in the first half of our lives? How is it possible to impose a single way of thinking over every maturing adult's evolving intellectual brain today? This is another perfect example of how our programming, including our unconscious need to belong and our need for safety and security, automatically reacts and overrides our thinking.

Let's go deeper: Conformity means there is a *'one rule fits all'* Pack philosophy and the status quo is *never* about the individual or individual freedom.

***

As you move closer to your freedom, you will be:

- Seeking cooperation and reconciliation between old beliefs and behaviours and your current needs.

- Transitioning a black-or-white, either/or world into grey areas of choices, negotiation and conciliation.

- Transcending fear-based comfort zones to expand and progress your personal development.

- Transforming emotional dependence and conformity into emotional *in*dependence and free will – the adult's rite of passage.

You are taking adult responsibility for yourself and giving yourself permission and the authority that is commensurate with that responsibility.

Those who step away from the status quo are often labelled… the troublemakers, the misfits, the degenerates and the rebels of society. *Given the system we were born into, it's an understandable status quo response, isn't it?* But it's usually those 'labelled' individuals who make the revolutionary/evolutionary changes in life. They should be applauded and cheered on, not discouraged and ridiculed.

I'd like to add here: if we go our own way, we will be judged! In fact, expect to be judged. We learnt to judge because we were judged in the first half of our lives. It's the repetition of generational cycles again. Don't take their comments personally; no harm meant… just judgements.

Also realise: it's never about you! The people who oppose you or resist your idea or message or a change in your behaviour, are living by their beliefs! Remember, *they don't like change of any kind.* They are scared, security conscious people who are protecting themselves and their position. They treat everyone who show signs of dissident behaviour as a potential threat to their innate need for security and certainty.

Understand also: the status quo will rarely change… only if it feels the weight of their membership to do so. You will be fighting their rules for the rest of your life. If you want more or something different, you must make it happen for yourself.

Who makes you feel disempowered? How do they benefit from disempowering you?
....
....
....

How do you feel disempowered? When?
....
....
....

What do you do with your frustration? E.g., do you become angry with yourself? Do you give up, settle? Do you go to the gym? Any others?
....
....
....

Conformity clipped our wings in the first half of our lives, but today, maturing individuals have the freedom to transcend their learnt behaviours and fly.

Are you ready to forge your own path and live congruently with your maturing needs? How will your life be different? What will you change?

....
....
....

One more thing:

There is a conscious art to knowing how far you can push the boundaries with a person, a group or an institution that is on a different frequency and life path to you. When you get to this level in your understanding, you will realise you don't need to ask anyone for permission or their approval. You are free to take the initiative and decide the best way to live your life... beyond traditional learnt conformity.

There is a Section devoted to 'The Establishment' and the chain gang, in my book: 'Defiance – Secrets of your midlife crisis.'

25. WHAT IS PERSONAL POWER?

We are now in a place in time, with an evolving intellect, where we can choose individuality and personal power above primitive survival programs, 'the Pack' and its conforming mentality. Let's find out how personal power conducts itself:

Personal power:

- has no concerns about what others may think of you.

- whether they think of you at all!

- is free from fear, bullying and all external influences.

Personal power is independent and free thinking, associated with free will, choices and the right to be yourself. It is the consummate grown-up act of choosing to live by your own Code of behaviour – an empowered adult, congruent with your stage of life and your maturing needs – liberating emotional dependence and conformity issues from your childhood and teenage 'belonging' years.

Personal power lives quietly and peacefully within the person who has ventured back to 'the self' and has given himself permission and the authority to take full responsibility for himself.

26. REINTERPRETING THE 'MIDLIFE CRISIS'

My explanation will involve some repetition, but please bear with me as this deeper explanation has been written to make even more sense of your life.

How did 'stuckness' affect me?
I remember feeling anxious, confused and overwhelmed. I was looking for direction. It was a short, but very disruptive time in my life. What made it worse was that I had no forewarning or understanding of what was really happening.

What is 'stuckness'?
We feel stuck in old patterns, learnt coping behaviours, beliefs, attitudes and the fear of moving away from familiar territory and comfort zone boundaries.

Where are we stuck?

- We are stuck in our learnt behaviours and conditioning.

- Stuck in childhood fear-based comfort zones.

- Stuck in old coping behaviours such as avoidance and blaming.

- Stuck in the 'black-or-white, 'yes-or-no', either/or world of a child.

- Stuck in our teenage generation's conformity issues.

- Stuck in our need for acceptance above self-acceptance.

Any others?

....
....
....

Why are we feeling stuck?

When our intellectual brain took over around the age of seven-years-old, our feeling/emotional life was given secondary importance and has remained on hold:

- By the age of 21, we are physically fully developed.

- Our intellectual brain continues evolving until around 25 years.

- Now our emotional life (right side brain) wants to catch up to *her* fully developed physical and evolving intellectual counterparts, giving us choices that expand our world and move us into the adult rite of passage… if we have the courage.

Your emotional life is the backbone of your life.
***She*, your right-side emotional brain, is your courage.**
***He*, your left-side intellectual brain, is your reasoning.**

Now, in midlife:

We've been conditioned to think that if we go against the status quo and its 'Pack' mentality, then we must be having a midlife crisis! *Not true… never been true!*

***

We have outlived the primitive, reactive/kneejerk survival system. We have outgrown our conditioning and all its rules, conforming and fitting in as we did in the first half of our lives. Midlife has no rules! Today, 'The individual' is free to claim his heroic and rightful place in history, choosing self-acceptance, personal power and free will above the need for acceptance, status quo conformity expectations and its forces of mediocrity.

***

ANOTHER BIG REASON TO INCLUDE YOUR FEELINGS:

When you dismiss the value of your emotional life, you become disconnected from your inner life. Your intellect bases its information on outside sources. If you haven't included your feelings in the decision making, *how do you know if the decision is the right one for you?* I know my 'intellectual only' decisions eventually became increasingly difficult and frustrating to live with. My life felt empty and stressed rather than filled with passion and purpose.

This is another reason why so many people change careers and lifestyles in midlife. They are done with the 'intellectual only' life and are going after a passionate and more emotionally satisfying life. They are incorporating and trusting their feelings and their powerful solar plexus chakra 'soul' connection, resonating and confirming their new direction.

Remember, your intellect is the new kid on the block – it had no part in your survival and still doesn't – the subconscious does most of the work in the first seven years, as it always has and as it aways will!

When we don't include all three powerbases i.e., physical, emotional and intellectual, we feel out of balance and disconnected with ourselves.

I believe this is why we seek comfort in drugs, comfort in alcohol, comfort in food and/or comfort in excessive amounts of sex. (You may disagree with the latter).

I know when I'm out-of-balance, I feel:

- disconnected from my physical self

- disconnected from my emotional life

- with only my over-functioning, overloaded intellect running the show, I go to the pantry and/or to the fridge. I'm not admitting to any others ☺

To harmonise with those three systems, try giving each a say in your day-to-day transactions with yourself.

It doesn't get better than this! From the moment we are born, we are blessed with everything working for us, always in our best interests, always looking after us helping us survive when we understand 'The system' and 'How life works'.

MY EXAMPLE OF PASSION, EMOTIONAL INDEPENDENCE AND COURAGE:

In 2017, I bought a Mustang 5.0 litre, V8 fastback coupe. It was one of the most heroic moments in my life. I'll never forget it! You boys have no idea! I had to accelerate over many fear-based generational speed humps such as 'Why would a woman (of your age) buy a muscle car?' and 'Mustang Sally'… OMG!

UNDERSTAND THE DIFFERENCE:

- The act of buying my Mustang was *never* about a midlife crisis.

- My purchase was *never* to upset anyone or to go against 'The Pack'.

- I did it for me! I was exercising my adult freedom to choose. Simple!

You may like to re-read 'Conformity' in Section III to reinstate the aware adult Empowered Concepts.

REINFORCING… NO SUCH THING AS A MIDLIFE CRISIS:

Superficially, when we see anyone with greying hair buying a sports car or a muscle car, it does look like delinquent adult behaviour, doesn't it? But what is really happening is those courageous maturing adults are transcending their fear of rejection, making heroic choices that embrace their emotional independence, personal power and free will. *We should salute their gutsy, proactive behaviours.*

Your V8 power is also found under the bonnet i.e., in your inner life. It is the adult's rite of passage to make choices that work in your best interests today – *with or without status quo approval.* Slowly… one tiny step at a time… be bold!

Any 'ah-ha' moments for you? How will you use your new insights?
....
....
....

What will you add to your courage shopping list? ☺

....

....

....

27. 'THE INDIVIDUAL' AND ITS PLACE IN HISTORY

Herds of sheep, schools of fish, flocks of birds, groups of people – all species live under Universal programs for the survival of life.

We have been dependent on others to feel okay about ourselves since we were children and teenagers. Until we have upgraded our adult self-image, our feelings of self-worth today are based on other people's opinions of us and/or their reactions to us from a different time zone. Fitting in, 'following the leader' and the concept of safety in numbers was a perfectly reasonable and appropriate response in the first half of our lives.

Now… when we don't understand 'The system', our innate 'Need to belong' continues to *un*consciously laud it over us, undermining 'The individual' today. Trying to live with *'what will my family and friends think?'* or *'what will the neighbours say?'*, fearing rejection, 'stuck' in subconscious automatic reactions, all lead to feelings of powerlessness, frustrating our attempts to fulfill our potential as a maturing individual in this time zone.

It's always been the same: There are stories throughout history about black sheep, aren't there? Breakaway painters, artists, architects, to modern day reformists have always been considered the rebels, the outcasts, the degenerates and problems for Society who wanted to shut them up or shut them down.

Fortunately, the human species with its evolving intellectual brain can acknowledge and transcend these programs, no longer 'dumbed down' and stunted by a survival system that was created for a lifespan, no longer than 35 years.

Now you understand 'The system' and why it has been so difficult for the individual:

**Welcome to the adult's rite of passage.
Be inspired... become an inspiration.**

***

Thank you:

Power to 'The individual' – to you and the little kid in you! May you live up to your new image and your awesome new 'dream-team' possibilities. Best wishes, courage and phenomenal success.

I would like to finish this Section with a tribute to your inner child, lovingly and responsibly renamed your subconscious 'Backseat driver'. Please read or listen to this tribute a couple of times so it really talks to you.

A TRIBUTE TO THE INNER CHILD

"I love my inner child's primal simplicity –
Her beliefs in the first seven years created our history.
My inner child believes she is all she can be…
She is the younger version of me.

I see everything through my inner child's eyes…
Her beliefs become my beliefs until I am wise.
She is dependent and powerless in *every* way –
I show her there's more when I 'shoo' fear away.

With her by my side I make perfect sense…
She is the substance, the heart and the core of my essence.
Our 'dream-team' consciousness transforms my identity.
I am complete and transcending my inner child's destiny."

Louise L. Kallaway.

Notes:

CONSCIOUS - 'How life works'...

ADDENDUM – THE FAMILY –
it all starts here!

You are now aware that every child's inner child is establishing its unique childhood model of life. It is an unconscious, trusting acceptance that whatever it is learning and observing in the first seven years of its life is real, true and correct and the way life is and the way it will always be... according to the literal child.

Children are being shown how their new world works, especially inside the family unit. What are they learning?

- Think about the words and expressions you use when talking to or disciplining a child, or in the earshot of a child. *What are they hearing?*

- Think about the behaviour you and other members of your family are displaying. What are the children learning and observing from you? *What are they seeing?*

- Think about how children feel about themselves and their capabilities in your presence. *What are they feeling?*

This information is being stored in their childhood model, resulting in enduring, future subconscious reactions and responses – what you are now trying to unravel and overcome in your maturing years!

I would also like to include teenagers here. Teenagers are not rebelling! They are transitioning from the tribal family to their generation for acceptance. They are growing up! In this confusing time, they need your support and understanding more than ever. Please remember that your comments live on in their subconscious image of themselves.

Let's disrupt the unconsciousness of repeated generational cycles. Be mindful of your truly powerful position. We are more enlightened now. We can do better for the generations who follow us.

Family respect:

There seems to be a reluctance in some family units – whether they be tribal or immediate – to change with the times. This creates a widening and deepening chasm between the progress being made in the outside world and the lack of change happening within 'old' family structures.

Respect and dignity are the two prerequisites to building a healthy relationship. Without respect, what do we base our relationships upon?

Open the conversation around the dinner table when most, if not all, the family members are present. Bring the above information to the dinner table conversation. Say what needs to be said. Communication is the hallmark of healthy relationships. Clear the air. Speak up on matters within your family that are creating dissension. Are the adults setting a great example for your children, showing how families negotiate and conciliate their differences and end the day in harmony?

Would you like your children to replicate any behaviours they are seeing in your family and the wider family circle? These are fair questions, especially when you consider the amount of feral behaviour, fear and violence being reported in some family units.

We know the phrase, 'Do as I say, not as I do!' falls on deaf ears. Children are copycats! The behaviours children are seeing repeatedly will be repeated unconsciously to future generations. Are there any behaviours in your family circle that are potentially damaging, creating the relationship problems of tomorrow and the next generation? Does each member of the family acknowledge the uniqueness of the other? – no matter their gender, age or position. Does each family member feel a sense of importance and dignity; that the family is a place of safety, respect and love?

Time to break another cycle.

***

Domestic violence is usually considered physical violence, but abuse has many tentacles. An equally powerful one, in my view, is emotional abuse – controlling, 'stirring', sniggering, sniping and ridiculing an individual. This type of abuse is felt on a deep and emotional level; *the untold damage to the psyche, self-esteem and self-worth coming through emotionally painful counselling sessions years later and perpetuating similar behaviours in the next generations before the cycle is broken.*

***

The women's movement cannot go backwards. When we look at all the areas women are involved in, consummate in, all the multi-tasking that goes on to run a family and even more so when we are going to work every day, we cannot think of ourselves as diminutive and unimportant. We are acknowledging our need for respect and self-respect, expecting more of ourselves and more of our relationships, including family relationships. This expectation continues to grow and refuses to be ignored.

Having a family unit that does not observe and embrace this changing face of society makes it difficult to fit in within the framework of family structures that passed their 'use by' decades ago.

We need to challenge family model basics and work with changing values, and, at the same time, review and liberate old generational issues. No-one will think less of the family hierarchy taking a democratic rather than a dictatorial role. In fact, that move will no doubt bolster their position, demonstrating a bold new attitude and a progressive new vision for the future of families.

***

Respectful relationships:

When you decide what someone wants or needs, above what they have decided for themselves, *you are creating problems for them!* Conversely, when others decide what you want when you have already stated what is right for you, *they are creating the problem, making your life more difficult!*

To compound the problem further, the situation is usually taken personally by the advisor/challenger, blaming the other – who is making his own choices – as the bad guy!

We need to step back and allow 'the other' to make their own choices, above what we believe is right for them. This also applies to the parents of adult children.

Is peace on earth getting closer?

ABOUT THE AUTHOR:

Hello there! My interest and fascination into 'The system' we were born into began in my difficult teenage years.

My Mum and her little brother, aged 4 and 3 respectively, were made Wards of the State in New South Wales, Australia, during the Great Depression. Abruptly taken from their family home, remembering abandonment is a primal fear to a child, you can imagine the two little kids' terror and confusion as they were passed to an unknown and unfamiliar carer. I would love to give them a big hug and assure them, wouldn't you?

I remember asking my Mum when I was 16, *"Why did you bring us up the same way you were brought up when it hurt you so much?" "How else was I supposed to bring you kids up? It's the only way I know!"* was her emotional retort!

My curiosity was piqued. My 16-year-old's question: *'how can I prevent history repeating itself?'* became my adult question: *'Why do generational cycles repeat themselves?'* Thirty years later, the last pieces in life's giant jigsaw completed the puzzle!

***

I want you to know: when I began my research, I had no idea that my discoveries would disrupt anything! I simply wanted to understand why my mother repeated her harsh and insensitive childhood to her innocent children, so I wouldn't automatically repeat my upbringing to my innocent kids.

***

Over time it has become increasingly apparent that acceptance of my research would mean a complete overhaul, update and re-education to many tertiary qualifications, including mental health and early childhood development, among others. To ignore evolving discoveries and to pretend this research does not exist, is what the status quo does. No offense intended – that's its job! – continuing to keep us safe, living within 'The Pack' and its *united we stand, divided we fall*' mentality, maintaining 'order' and resisting change of any kind and so… perpetuating mediocrity. We remain part of the status quo when we choose to be silent, above making a difference in our community or by making better or more empowering choices for ourselves.

Without people like you who are willing to investigate new research and new possibilities, the world will remain stagnant in the hands of the status quo. If this Journal has helped make sense of your life, imagine how it could help people with depression, anger issues, suicidal thoughts, feelings of 'stuckness' and powerlessness etc.

If you think the world is ready, would you like to start a Movement with me? … to promote awareness of the 'survival system' we inherited and to evolve the parent/child dynamic to advance future generations.

I may be contacted at www.linkedin.com/in/louise-l-kallaway-57b667198/ or through my website: louiselkallaway.com

***

FYI, My book *Evolving – Secrets of a child and life processes* was awarded three amazon.com #1 bestseller distinctions in three categories alerting parents and carers of young children to the survival system and the two time zones.

Having difficulty locating any of my 'Life education' books or journals? Please go to my website where you can order direct. Thank you again, Louise.

www.ingramcontent.com/pod-product-compliance
Lightning Source LLC
Chambersburg PA
CBHW050819090426
42737CB00021B/3440